Also by William Allen

The Man on the Moon
(New York University and Persea Presses), 1987

Sevastopol: On Photographs of War
(Xenos Press), 1997

North Passage
(Clay Street Press), 2019

The Largest Glue Factory in the World
(Spuyten Duyvil), 2024

A History of the Azores
(Clay Street Press), 2025

The Birth of the Atlantic

William Allen

Spuyten Duyvil
New York City

ISBN 978-1-969900-20-4
Cover photo by Tasha Marie, 2022 on Unsplash
Back cover photo by Santiago Yanez, 2021 on Unsplash

Library of Congress Control Number: 2026943937

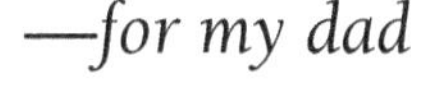

—for my dad

Contents

Part One: Home
The Birth of the Atlantic 15
Tea at Habib's 16
Corner Seventh and Avenue A 17
Dutch Kills 18
St. Mark's Poetry Project 20
Ocean Parkway 21
Charlie Parker Place 23
On Sojourner Truth Day 25
Old Farm Road 26
Pokanoket Powwow 27
Twilight, Tudor City 28

Part Two: Dreams
Montauk Blue 31
Horse News 32
Hyper-objects 33
Thimble Island Ocean Farm 34
Coronavirus Poem 35
Sunken Playground 37
After Ashbery 38
On Entropy 39
Horn & Hardart Automat 40
Dinosaur Trackway, Rocky Hill 41
721 Fifth Avenue 42

Part Three: Pilgrimage

Cahokia 45
Fallingwater 47
Three Rivers Petroglyphs 48
Grand Canyon, North Rim 49
Bitter Lake 50
In Bethlehem 51
Volkspark Hasenheide 52
Notre-Dame du Haut, Ronchamp 53
TV Garden, TV Buddha 54
Addis Ababa 55
Ayutthaya 57

Part Four: History

The Age of Moss 61
The Great Flowering 62
Toba Bottleneck 63
Sassafras 64
Little Ice Age 65
History of the Palatines 66
Poplar Forest 68
The Oblong 70
The Goblet of the Titans 72
Hudson, Whaling City 73
Earth Day, 2024 74

Part Five: Nature
Salamander Crossing 77
The Thirteenth Lake 78
Landscape, Three Cows 79
Cicadas 80
Out Eeling 81
Soundscape Pando 82
On the Esopus 83
Reading Mary Oliver 84
Capybara Ocean 85
Clouds 86
The Far Field 87

Acknowledgements 95
About the Author 96

A poem is an action of the mind captured on a page. It is a movement of yourself through a thought, through an activity of thinking, so by the time you get to the end you're different than you were at the beginning.

Anne Carson

Poetry is a place where both grief and grace can live, where rage can be explored and examined, not simply exploited.

Ada Limón

Plato the Greek or Rin Tin Tin, who's more famous to the billion millions?

The Clash

Hello from the children of planet earth

Nick Sagan, age six, Voyager Golden Record

Part One: Home

The Birth of the Atlantic

There may be more beautiful times, but this one is ours.
Jean-Paul Sartre

Pangea breaks apart—as methane gases
gush from hydrothermal vents.
The Appalachians, then as tall
as the Himalayas tower now,
crumble into a sea that rushes in,
like an oncoming tsunami,
calving the Atlas Mountains,
Africa and Europe. Ancestor eels
must migrate either east or west
across the virgin waters
of the Gulf Stream,
up past plumes to Iceland.

Our families came from Scotland,
Brittany, but we two sit across the sea
from there as friends, watching whales
swim by the New York Battery.

—for Norman MacAfee (1943-2024)

Tea at Habib's

First, we drink a Turkish coffee and discuss
the end of physics, an art crowd we invited
to our storefront. Punks out front shatter
panes of glass because they can, we settle
with a homeless veteran for sweeping up.

We drag our kids to the swimming pool
at Tompkins Square, where suddenly, all
at once, a kindergartner floats face down
in the water, with little impulse to live on.

We shake her, take her to Habib—who's
smiling like a gentleman—we bring her
back to life with sugar in a glass of tea,
Louis Armstrong on and miles of Miles,
the syncopated jazz that keeps us going.

Corner Seventh and Avenue A

The old man on the corner was Ukrainian,
he wore a crimped, oily paper bag as a hat
and sat out here through winter fires, vodka
shots and riots in the park. Though he often
lost sight of the trees beyond the fountain,
his fingers always fiddled—twisting, rolling,
bending, reinventing toothpicks, scrimshaw,
cigarettes, anything that could be scrawled
upon or twiddled. His swollen hands were
always empty and only once over the years
did I ever see him eat—some chicken fried
rice in a battered tinfoil pan. He didn't speak
to us or look in our direction, his lips were
always moving, muttering, murmuring, as if
forging whispers in the air, done in a strange
tongue to emphasize that he was here to stay.

Dutch Kills

The day I moved to New York City, the skies
were overcast, Allen Ginsberg was up at night
scribbling paeans to a bird, a smell of jasmine
permeated sidewalk cracks on Second Avenue.
In 1980, people walking, talking to themselves
were displaced persons—or maybe journalists
waiting for a word from Mayakovsky. Punks,
political, slept at after-parties on the Bowery.
My pen pal from Cologne arrived to visit me,
she buttoned me up in snap-on ties to walk
in Loisaida gardens, meander with a pinhole
camera to a day job tabulating science grades
on high school tests for nurses, ex-offenders,

when my approach to language was to listen.
The moon shone bright, I worked weekends
on a tug in Jersey City, dreaming at midnight
of a man on a ferry in the Newtown Creek,
where he slogged away, side by side with me
on poems by the inky waters of Dutch Kills.
A poet on a boat? Intrigued, I kept Camus
close by, went out on dates with socialists
before I knew of Bernie Sanders, Mamdani
or AOC. The bikeable roads propelled me
to a rusty bascule bridge on Borden Avenue.
Years later, my daughter lived in Greenpoint,
we helped with cleaning up a toxic waste that

seeped heating oil into a street of sumac trees.
Eventually, the evolution of a treatment plant
included a percentage for the arts, an eco-trail,
finally extended to a Whale Creek turret cone
that commemorated organisms of early Earth.
The artist Trakas thought of everything, where
sump digesters kept crud or ooze from leaking
into wetlands. The cemeteries spoke the loudest,
we could hear banshees all the way to Rockaway.
I went to spoken word soirees at Milk & Roses,
drank dark red Reserva, studied Goya's etchings
as tiny nightjars slept. Back home on Fifth St.
my studio was so packed with maps I couldn't

see the floor to sweep it. And then Covid came,
we dreamt cabbages, pierogis, being twenty-one
again or wrestling with an angel (Sam) who met
me at Dutch Kills to wander up pollinator paths
of daisy, purslane, by plaques on prehistoric life
and a nomadic family who domesticated dogs.
With fire in the air, I thought I knew the world,
began to understand my limits and my friends.
When the Clash played at CBGB's, Patti Smith
became my favorite heroine. Sunday worship
meant discovering the skimmers, sludge boats,
fossil trees from the terrifying age of fishes,
a world without end, a second kingdom come.

St. Mark's Poetry Project

We come to celebrate a land where poetry is as
commonplace as washcloths, paint cans, banana milk,
as we curse our funding of a government of thugs
and hit squads, as sinkholes swallow buses,
umbrellas, bakeries. We translate stories
from the tin-can towns, where people
queue around a stucco house for bread.

I read a poem about a pier and ocean,
a crate of oranges, an elegy to sun, someone
painting seagulls. The room is full of listeners,
keen to hear what I could not say, words about
a decomposing mole, the double of a friend
whose spirit came to me before he died.

I join poets for a New Year's marathon,
on deck just after Bernadette, as cats climb up
the belfry, as strangers pace a widow's walk,
as an outdoor concert booms an insane hope
for a theology of liberation, a box of socks
from you in Germany onstage with me
as I sing of longing for our special place.

Ocean Parkway

I'm biking the last mile to Coney Island,
Agee's *Brooklyn Is* is in my backpack as
I gobble down tamales and sail off into
a city's restless river of outbound traffic.
Uzbek men play chess upon a boulevard

of elms set out by Olmsted, as I happen
on a poet friend who's moving cars from
one side of the parkway to the other, as a
black pawn takes a queen. We can't sleep,
we live above a kiosk, B23 buses grinding

to a halt and ambulances wailing off to
hospitals. We buy a sound machine with
television static, thunder, ocean breakers,
as teens play noisy video games till 4 a.m.
The horse parade grounds are a greenway

for parrots building nests on phone poles.
Boys visit us from Ruidoso, where there
are no aquariums or eels. All night long
along allées, ailanthus trees are burning,
a cement plant by an F train is churning

out concrete by a nightmare postal stop.
Kids from Tel Aviv and Gaza City share
their lunch, a fish plaque near Cortelyou
portrays a codfish. We spot the words
'of frozen snow' on a supermarket wall.

A stone's throw to Sheepshead Bay, a cab
ride to Canarsie, Ocean Parkway sparkles.
On moving-in day, we were very pleased,
as our landlady with freshly painted nails
was panicking, *Take the keys! Take the keys*!

Charlie Parker Place

We sit outside the Life Cafe with a squirmy
toddler, under a locust tree near Avenue B,
a reddish glare of morning sun on what's left
of migrant camps, urban rangers, squad cars.
The park wakes up to people drinking coffee,
a crowd of hungry neighbors at Saint Brigid's.

We celebrate the birthday of our little one,
bebop blaring from a horseshoe bar inside,
pages of a Daily News plastered on a wall,
sprays of gladioli everywhere. A helicopter
passes low to photograph some protesters.
Rastafarians arrive, a rooster crows behind

the library where I have my studio, asking
writers in a workshop what inspires them,
not surprised by what they say: molecules,
mind games, chat rooms, adobe mosques
in Mali and Charlie Parker's 'Ornithology.'
He lived across the street from here! one barista

from Detroit exclaims, as she is finishing
her story about the man whose rhythms,
she likes to say, mimic catbirds in a fever
pitch, up on the roof, with a natural flow
on a saxophone that lights up everything
about to happen in this corner of a world,

from frenzied car alarms, bucket drumming,
sirens and air horns across a canopy of oaks.
His life in E flat major, with manic intervals
of chords as melody, where 'Bird' would play
the thing he heard. Most of all, Charlie Parker
was a warbler, wailing, riffing, railing, running

free, like Klee's *Twittering Machine*, like music
of the trees, where robins congregate inside
his rhythmic arc, each phrasing ending on
an offbeat, like a veery singing two scales
at once, rising, falling, deeply reedy, eerie,
as in *Out of Nowhere*, *Straight, No Chaser*, five

or six years of practice fifteen hours a day
in the Ozark woods. Here his brownstone
resounds in shadows of a skinny sycamore.
Listening, we close our eyes, lose all sense
of self, just enjoy a chattering of children
before we soar towards home in bird flight.

On Sojourner Truth Day

But man is in a tight place, the poor slave is on him, woman is coming on him, he is surely between a hawk and a buzzard.

It's Sojourner Truth Day in New York State,
as I try to remember the saints' names' days,
from lady astronauts to Gold Star Mothers,
Ella Fitzgerald, Mother Theresa, Rosa Parks,
Greta Garbo and Sacagawea. I keep a pack

of U.S. postage stamps with their likenesses,
my heart is swelling with their simple words.
We hike the hollowed quarry named for her,
by cracked, concrete slabs, brick-kilns, ice
huts on the river, where she was born a slave

and fought to free her children, suffragettes,
African American tradesmen and truck farm
hands from Savannah with their backs to a
moldboard plow for forty acres and a mule.
On the hill where a creek trickles down,

we point our walking sticks, count out fauna
that live in the wetlands. Beavers don't think
of freedom, jays don't read the Constitution,
but even the way this noisy waterfall cascades
to a lagoon is democratic. My hand is, too.

Orchard bees, awash in wind-borne pollen
are democratic, as is your kiss, your touch,
your one more moment of truth. Can we try
to celebrate today by visiting the frog pond
and try to come across a hawk or buzzard?

Old Farm Road

A tractor tows a brush hog up and down
the bluestem meadow in a glacial till that
once was full of bluebirds, burdock, hay.
When I was young, I walked here with
my dad and his one-armed Navy SEAL
pal bent on making a life from furrows
of the earth, where red potatoes grow,

where crows nest high above the corn.
Now I hike alone, finding on muddied
paths a stand of cattails, burrs and ticks
as well as sorrows of the heart laid out
by a wedding party that's visiting from
Queens, under cirrus clouds that seem
almost one-dimensional, as the groom

heads home uphill. Towhees scratch
or trill from the bushes by a cow path,
past a dairy barn and silos on the old
farm road, now fantastically overgrown
in ripe, red raspberries. I can't stop myself
from crawling in the prickers and picking
gobs of them to eat and then to use as ink.

Pokanoket Powwow

Drumbeats draw us to the center
of a group of chanting celebrants
at a powwow in Pawtucket. Bells

hang down from cypress trees, as
jays take flight to mob a barn owl.
Bonfires, beads, a flatbed pickup.

Basket-makers sort their wares
to smells of burning ash or soot.
Children peep on wooden flutes,

we sit by an entrance to the cedar
swamp where warriors once slept
and their sachem kept her council.

Friends have come from the city
to visit Metacomet's forest chair
on the anniversary of his killing,

deep in woods where we picnic
on a rock, read from the removes,
a tribute to the many disappeared.

Now we try to see faces in the fire
as elders leap with staffs in hand
and the summer sun begins to set.

Twilight, Tudor City

I'm happy at the park, reading my way to Circe's
cave, poring over notes on gardening, user guides
for mountaineers, botanists, alchemists who look
to differentiate a good life from something else
or tell the tale of insect metamorphosis, the joys

of growing up, getting older, maybe navigating
by the stars. It's just past the summer solstice,
after work at sunset, as line cooks, doormen,
cabbies, demonstrators gather on the bridge,
the sun aligning with the street grid, setting

42nd Street on fire to reveal our Stonehenge.
No need to say any more. Future beings will
surely know from our remains that the culture
honored Pepsi, iron ore and battleships galore.

Part Two: Dreams

Montauk Blue

We drive to a motel at the edge of paradise,
late in October on a day when the hardware

stores have boarded up their louvre doors.
The wind is picking up, an ambulance idles

as the moon goes pale, rising over breakers
that crash into shoals of a continental shelf,

where jellyfish float above the luminescence.
We huddle on the balcony, where the crash

of surf is overwhelming every pulse of fear,
of joy, togetherness. We hear Bob Dylan on

the radio, as if we'd slipped back fifty years
in time. And here we are, listening to the end.

Horse News

The local paper says a horse went crazy,
hitting a motorcyclist on Violet Avenue.
Do horses fly? Ask Arion or Bucephalus.
Aging Percherons chew clover, as ghostly
roans race across the Badlands nightly, as
a headless horseman sizes up the moon.
Buttermilk played her part in Hollywood,

zebras on the loose in Clinton Corners.
Bolivar rode his horse up Machu Picchu
while Rosinante sparred with windmills.
A mare has caught the equine influenza,
her colts take antitoxins for diphtheria.
In a wood where we live, ponies canter.
Across the world, stallions dream alfalfa.

Hyper-objects

Morton thinks it means a plastic garbage patch,
fields of fossil footprints, black holes, beaches,
a grease pool in Greenpoint as well as alligators
in the Everglades. A biosphere, a giant network
of a quaking aspen tree, a particulate of carbon
discovered in an ant or polar satellites that orbit
the Earth. Every last Paris shoestring, viscous,

molten, phased, quashed, it's a poem that starts
with lullabies, spins out in traffic on the widest
boulevard in Maspeth. They were here before
we conquered fire, multiplied across the globe
in hungry tribes, till now when every other word
is about a body or a self. For me, a hyper-object
is as simple as a hot tar that bubbles in the street.

Thimble Island Ocean Farm

Dad had disappeared, Mom's just
come back from Tijuana, Mexico
to finalize the paperwork and find
a path to start afresh, with kids to
feed and clothe and keep in school.
We drive to the Lyme stone church
where we heard that JFK was shot.

We visit our father in his rental by
the sound, where the only sounds
are inter-city trains, grasshoppers
clamoring to make a claim on our
confusion and lack of self-esteem.
I return to Stony Creek in a dream
of Thimble Islands glistening, true

beacons of becoming. Now we have
to practice a philosophy of kelp for
the ocean farms, for worlds of water,
a next-gen engine of everything that's
good, generous, or giving, one way to
compromise, economize, revolutionize
our people, our planet, our happy few.

Coronavirus Poem

The semi-tractor trailer trucks are lining up
at Elmhurst Hospital, just a block from us,
to carry out the dead. We curl into balls in
a dim, one-bedroom and wait to hear from

doctors who are muffled voices in the dark.
I meet our daughter at the Newtown Creek
on a cold day in the sun, both on bikes, not
ready to touch or probe too deeply what

the past two weeks have been, her mom
too ill to go out—but still we try to focus.
We can't smell or taste—and the buses, now
not charging fees, gather germs from every

corner of the globe. Masked, terrified, we
try to find an open market near our home.
We rent a car and pile some things inside,
drive from Queens to Brooklyn to pick up

baby wipes, fly through the Battery tunnel,
racing away from what's invisible. Clouds,
fire trucks along an interstate to Westerly
and beyond—where the military stops us

in our tracks to double check that we are
passing through. At a Cape Cod bridge,
a hundred Trumpers are rallying against
the empty wind. We travel on to camp

in a cabin by the sea. We find noon's
solace, despite the news of my cousin's
heart attack and others we don't know
in ICUs. We unfurl a bit in April 's cold

as we watch the body count keep rising,
as Covid grips a nation and the planet.
My mom is over ninety now, celebrates
her birthday from the hospice window,

a bunch of us below by blooming pear
trees with a poster saying *we love you!*
Gulls hover above us in a sky of blue.
We wear masks, get vaccinations, begin

to heal from being split in pieces. Our
daughter walks each sunset to the river
to name the ospreys and the clams. We
sleep well, share a hope for a better day.

Sunken Playground

Airbus jets careen across the sunrise in
the Heights, yellow ginkgos, sycamores
surround me. A fading blast of a passenger
train—five cars long with sleepy commuters
who dream of palaces of fire—along its way
to 125th Street, after trauma and a tragedy.
Here in Audubon's orchard is his final
resting place, orioles announce a morning
for the nursing staff at Presbyterian, where
you lie in wait to get a word on living or
on dying. Up a retaining wall, Francisco
Alarcón has splayed in green *but my soul*
is even darker from all the light I carry inside.
When I wake from this strange dream
of many days gone bad but blessed,
you are here with me, we've made it
through a nightmare in the surgery,
it's sunset in the sunken playground
and my heartbeat slows, so I can rest.

After Ashbery

Clouds converge above lush tulip fields
in Delft, here in Kinderhook, forests flush
with spongy moths, sprouting chestnuts.

The die is cast, we count our blessings,
we sit on boulevards of broken dreams
and think up games for a brood of kids
displeased with all the talk about disease.

What's left of secrets from Diderot's
encyclopedia on trades and industry?
Ask the witch on Haystack Mountain.

In a parking lot, you find a circuit board
that's perfect for your artwork—all you
have to do is plug it in with solar power
and the force of it will heat a city block.

On Entropy

I contemplate the wind, count carpenter
ants in a nonchalant parade from a melon
to a mildewed stump. My ears are buzzing
as I shoot down the Taconic, as it starts
to rain along the flooded railroad tracks.
By a silo, I spot lacewings in the milkweed,
recall that friends are a hundred miles away.
A glacial lake bleeds into blue mountains,

wildfires in Québec burn haze off heather,
tree frogs gag on smoke. Red blood cells in
my body fail faster than it can remake them.
Another rocket ship is heading off to Mars,
my car gets sap on it, the heat from a coffee
thermos dissipates while another economic
downturn shakes Japan. While my energy
is constant, the universe may soon collapse.

Horn & Hardart Automat

Our carful of children from New London
picks up foster kids in Harlem, where we
breakfast with the family, barrel down to
midtown in a white Ford Falcon, to tour
the United Nations, to eat at an automat
where you could order a BLT without a
waitress, from a forty-cent slot machine:

hamburger steak, sardine toast, macaroni,
tongue on rye or baked beans for a dollar.
Ted giggles as we prod each other's Jello,
daydream of a minister from Atlanta who
says that out of mountains of despair we
hew a stone of hope. A mystery in the air
about this promise on a day in May when

James Baldwin meets with Bobby Kennedy
as riots flare in Birmingham, finding a way
through peaceful protest, a brother weeping
at the body count in Vietnam. When I turn,
a city's vanishing in a station wagon window.
We're tired from the talking and the walking,
but all of us ready to meet the world head on.

Dinosaur Trackway, Rocky Hill

Jurassic, bird-like footprints in the fossil record here,
found when we were eight and six and four and two years old,
living right nearby. But no one took us to see the myriad of tracks,
though we spent weeks at home with plastic figurines that served
to animate those fierce and terrible lizards, vanished
in a flash before we had the wherewithal
to know where they had gone.

Summer afternoons were tropical in our back yard,
a fort in the forsythia our window into their rapacious past.
We loved their names, Allosaurus and Eubrontes,
feeding on the floodplains of our river valley.

In storm and molten wrack and lightning,
flocks of nervous, hungry dinosaurs would gather here
and thunder madly down the trackway after prey.

721 Fifth Avenue

In a dream (or was it real?), Melania wears Zara,
an army jacket saying *I Really Don't Care, Do U?*
while visiting a migrant child detention home
at a Texas border. And an orange-tufted louse
is cringing as they glide along a staircase bearing
chalices of Russian wine from the Ural steppes.
Across the vast expanse of an atrium of crystal
chandeliers, autoharps play switched-on Bach
while an Irish chef falls backwards off a beam
four stories into a roiling pool of silvery carp.
His thinning blood now circulates up and down
the dazzling waterfall, a crowning achievement
of the pair. The campaign for President has now
begun, with this offering to ensure a terrific run.

Part Three: Pilgrimage

Cahokia

North America's first city. Why did it vanish, almost overnight?
Did it follow the familiar arc of corruption and collapse?
Or was it a drought that came with the Little Ice Age?
We're on our yearly road trip, like all good citizens,
driving like there's no tomorrow in a red convertible,
headed to the Gateway Arch, as tall as it is wide,
on the Mississippi's banks, a midpoint in our lives,
discussing club drugs, teen angst, civil liberties,
panic eating, engineering, business opportunities,
a broken-windows theory of petty crime and bullying,
border wars, till we stop for lunch at the golden arches.

We think about the doors to East Berlin, Prague or Paris,
the Forbidden City, a soon-to-see delicate arch in Utah.
Lewis and Clark set out from here to reach the sea,
as we look down on a man-made wonder, gazing
at Cahokia, its mounds as tall as they are wide,
with shadows of a history of disappearances,
then a culture wholly gone. Early Mississippian,
grown too big for boundaries, woodhenge solstices,
its sweat lodge tributes in the form of human sacrifice,
trading salt, shells, beads, mica, chert or growing corn

and goosefoot, amaranth, canary grass, other starchy
seeds, storing surpluses for their wolf and eagle deities.
Wherever I walk, people from St. Louis stop me in
my tracks and want to talk (I wear a Cardinals cap)
as if the city was part and parcel of our destiny.
Like the Hohokam before them, Cahokians
were thriving one day and suddenly were gone,
dissolving into Chickasaw, Osage Nation, enduring
cracks and fissures in the soil, maybe even ecocide.
Maybe a shift in the tilt of the earth was enough to
silence all Cahokia, its mounds a portal to the future.

Fallingwater

I walked into a glade where solitary bees
were on the loose and architects dreamt
fast and furious, with sketches of castles
in the mists of Altamira, pinkish boughs
of rhododendron blooming everywhere.

Trombones blew down an oak right near
the entrance to Fallingwater, way out in
the Laurel Highlands, close to Shanksville,
where Jersey cows loitered in a meadow.

In the modernist house itself a green snake
slithered up a crevice to the roof. This was
proof enough for me that the music would
last forever, that I'd keep on careening west
until I reached black mounds of anthracite.

Three Rivers Petroglyphs

We drive through Carrizozo and the Tularosa Basin,
hundreds of stones with petroglyphs hold pictures
of the past: farmers of Jornada Mogollon thrived
for centuries here before Conquistadores came.
Then, in years of drought, they vanished overnight.

We walk trails, watch for rattlesnakes, San Andres
mountains glisten over gypsum mines or salt flats.
Years of family angst are peeling from our husks,
our kids, immune, dream broken pottery or kivas.
Painted rocks host circles, dots, as elk or antelope.

Once paradise on Earth, the desiccated dune fields
of White Sands Missile Base attract arroyo coyotes.
A trading post has baskets, mugs and MAGA caps,
not a single trace of people from Jornada Mogollon.
Clouds cast shadows of three rivers on a parking lot.

Grand Canyon, North Rim

We kids are in our army sleeping bags,
behind a Volkswagen camper, scattered out
in a ravine of prickly pear and million-year-old dust,
at the edge of a plateau.

Mom in tears—her life is shattering around her
as she gazes at the sky and a setting roseate sun.
A donkey brays, the desert ocean opens up.

Soon we're fast asleep, she has time to smoke,
brush her hair and mend her turquoise necklace,
as stars in Gemini spin off to keep us in their orbit.

Bitter Lake

It's the world of birds we turn to as we rebound
from hurricanes, forest fires and collective grief.
Refuge wetlands are a habitat for sandhill cranes
here in a Chihuahuan desert, where snow geese,
plovers and northern pintails jab at marsh grass.
It's not a tier in Dante's afterlife or hell—now
we're holding hands in forty years of marriage.

The bitter lake is beautiful. We're not the same
as we once were, nor have we changed one bit.
Sinkholes bubble up at every feeling wrought,
as we drive around the playa, and try to patch
the sore divisions of the night. Let the rest go,
we say, and try to forgive those things we can't
forget from our lives of struggle and surrender.

In Bethlehem

In Bethlehem, we visit the Church of the Nativity,
we walk along the Way of Sorrows, imagine a child
in a manger, with herds of sheep and Persian kings.
We take our coffee with a hint of cardamom—you
teach me words you've learned while working here.
Some things in Palestine just can't be said in English,
like how much water can be scooped up in a hand,
unwanted family obligations, a certainty from doubt,
a struggle to persist, the sound of brand-new clothes.
You tell me that *alcohol, algebra, candy, cotton,* and *elixir*
come from Arabic, as well as *hazard, shrub* and *tell.*
You say there is no word in English for *maktub,*
which means 'it's written,' as in the daily intifada,
'the shaking off' that's all around us or the thought
it might be fate that we're here together on this day.

Volkspark Hasenheide

At noon, atop a double-decker bus in Berlin,
I gaze at a television tower beyond the wall:
happy here, to find the center of the world.
We pass a ruined church, a stand of evergreens,
a bottle dump. Suddenly, out of the Volkspark
as if she were Brünnhilde, a towering woman
strides from the Hasenheide, perfectly naked,
past the Turkish and Croatian businessmen
sitting with smoked eel sandwiches, her arms
raised above her head as if to usher in the only
light the state of Brandenburg might offer us.
The bus dead-ends at once. Does she know
something that none of us who halt to gawk
at her can begin to know of the dance of life?

Notre-Dame du Haut, Ronchamp

High on a hill at Belfort, in eastern France, we make
a father-daughter day trip for the modern age, to the chapel
of Le Corbusier, to enjoy a sip of Malbec and Gruyère
before our jaunt to the mountaintop of monkeys.

It's June, the nearby farms are sleepy, we walk as if
through stations of the cross to seek the virgin
of the forest. Inside the church, a penitent has fallen
to the floor, she flails and weeps inside the nave.

Shades of the crusades and a German occupation,
the Jura mountains frame the pyramid of peace
where visitors are lunching in the grass. If you ask
us if we go to church, this is where we say we go.

TV Garden, TV Buddha

The first time I meet him he's poking in the trash
in Chinatown, picking at wooden produce crates
to make expressionist collage. One day he peers
down a Broome Street sidewalk sinkhole full
of gas lines, water mains and steam pipes,
awestruck at underground networks that gird
a city block, a power grid, an urban beehive.

At Canal and Mulberry, I pick up a Chinese
children's science book, on how plants drink.
We have coffee, stay friends for forty years,
he shows me video art that he's assembling,
Nam June Paik's 'TV Garden,' a low-tech nest
of forty picture tubes in a bed of succulents.
In a gallery corner, an introspective Buddha

sees himself in a loop of camera and a screen,
the only interference is the cloud of silence
as I dream we wander past it, set up shop
in the electronic forest of scheffleras, hiding
in undergrowth, watching Charlotte Moorman,
human cello, play Yoko Ono and ask an audience,
what order out of chaos lies beneath the streets?

—for Jochen

Addis Ababa

Full tilt, I race to lift two heavy women dressed in
flowing kemis who've fallen on an airport escalator.
Near the African Union, boys try to grab my cash.
I go for wedding cake at a Hyatt Regency, follow
a parade of children in bow ties who carry baby

desert animals. I rest from sprinting at the track
with friends, watching rotary traffic like amoebas
in a heat storm. I buy dry goods at an IT depot,
a corrugated roadside shack off Meskel Square
as a revolution of the Derg unfolds around us.

My friend from work escorts me to a fossil dig
and a communist museum, where we have spicy
chicken stew and beer. Later, horrid back pains
in a nightmare hostel room full of ghosts, as I
dream of early homo sapiens: a seven-year-old

scampering with a hoop by a very wet fire. Girls
catch scrub hares, a father skins them on a spit.
This could be you or me in another twenty years,
the same stars blinking above us. We drive out of
Addis Ababa, past flower stalls where women nap.

We've packed our tools for digging hominids and
gather a crew for a three-day trek into the vale
of tears, where *Australopithecus africanus* journeyed
far from home in search of meat and water, seed
sustenance for her growing tribe of wanderers.

With planets shifting over the Great Rift Valley,
we warm up by the fire, look out on a savannah
as our African ancestors did before us. It's dawn
when a pride of lions wakes, stretches, yawns
then circles sable antelopes gathered by the river.

—for Nebiyou Girma

Ayutthaya

We ride a sequined elephant, despite
the soaking rain in a city of three rivers.

A center of trade for Cambodians,
Thais, Burmese, we come to see

what's left of Siamese reliquary spires
and ancient heads of Bodhisattvas

grown into roots of trees. We know
that spirit cannot return to the body

after death, as younger monks walk
barefoot across a bridge of flowers.

We take a longboat down the Chao
Phraya River back to Bangkok, where

teens have sneakers, iPods, backpacks,
affirming that the third world's gone.

Grandfathers sport songbirds in cages
in a park where red silk cotton trees,

orchids, compete with Chincherinchee.
We pass by wats, moats, owls on leashes,

a milk-white Pomeranian in a hen's crate.
At the Bang pa-In Palace, I meet up

with middle-schoolers who just want
to hug me tight or practice their hellos.

They've all visited Ayutthaya, once or
twice on school trips, so they cry, but

they want to know about America, why
I say the best of it's around them here.

—for Shirin Hamid

Part Four: History

The Age of Moss

In the beginning, there was moss. Greenish algae slowly
shaped our life on earth, evolving into mass that blanketed
the landforms rising from the sea, with hairlike strands of filigree.
Imagine fastening to naked limestone cliffs, gazing at ocean
waves with sun and wind and air to breathe, no roots,
no dark entanglements of branches or thickened
leather leaves that sweat like poison ivy or magnolia,
your grasp on things as fragile as a sprig of moss.

To find your way home, just look for clumps that grow
on the north side of a tree. You'll find its stories sunk in bogs,
swamps or any habitat you see. There you might lie down
or become a stone. Moss will gobble up so much carbon
it's sure to bring about the next big mass extinction.
The very first plant on earth, moss may be the last.

The Great Flowering

Black birds stab at grass seed in the sod, or are they
after compost worms that squiggle into early spring,

spiders, mites or caterpillars creeping out of rotten
leaves that cover a backyard garden bed? Wrens check

out a nesting box, doing their due diligence, while
goldfinch greenies fill up on thistle. It's still a month

before we'll see a hummingbird, until the sturdy oaks
come fully into leaf. A pair of owls, a pair of great blue

herons, pairs are everywhere for this year's blossoming.
The world's first flower, a dwarf magnolia, opens wide

by the Yellow Sea in the Liaoning forest in Manchuria,
just like it did 130 million years ago, as if nothing much

has changed. Now angiosperms dominate the landscape.
Everywhere you look, some bud's exploding into bloom.

Toba Bottleneck

We meet on a boat in a caldera, once bubbling with molten lava
that belched out a decade-long volcanic winter across the seas,
a 1,000-year-long cooling spree, leading to a genetic bottleneck
in the human population, with only several thousand of us left.

It's conjecture (and may already be debunked), but it gives
me pause to think that as a species we almost didn't make it.
Out on the water, I start to remember things I knew before
I came into the world, including astral arts, a cure for AIDS

or cancer, why cats can land on four flat feet, how galaxies
might form and how to make a paper crane. And notably,
from the reservoir of all ideas, how did we survive a Toba
blast or how many of us will be here in the distant future?

Questions boil up to the surface of the lake, like why did
fruit bats here take to the air? Have you seen the upright-
walking *orang pendek*? Where is Malaysian Flight 370 now?
Or why can't science help deliver universal human rights?

We now extrapolate that in less than three hundred years
our numbers will veer back down from ten to two billion
people—not sure how many breeding pairs—those that
are left will have a feast of milk and honey. But there won't

be siamangs, binturongs, sun bears, pangolins or cuckoos,
by then a hazy smoke will be all that's left of any rainforest
in Sumatra or Sulawesi, but those of us who will be here
can canoe across Lake Toba to the monkey isle of Samosir.

Sassafras

In all these places, we saw no people but signes of
fires where they had beene.
The Voyage of Martin Pring, 1603

The tale begins with a need for sassafras, cedar planks,
one to cure the French pox (syphilis), another to build
more ships to travel to uncharted shores for plunder.
Before the Pilgrims got to Plymouth, Martin Pring
and crew were following the currents of Cape Cod,
where they found fishing grounds of Wampanoags,
who gathered there for oysters. Turkeys ran wild
as our imaginations do, as we harvest a bounty for
the elect, the errant in the wilderness, who, were
it not for some giant mastiff dogs, would have been
buried in a bog of cranberry. As it was, they survived,
gave no thanks, made no profits on their enterprise,
beat it back to England, then Guiana, then far east
and home at last to a Bristol churchyard in the heath.

Little Ice Age

Like Avercamps's skaters, we'd be out on the ice for hours
before anyone noticed that the winter sun was going down.
It was bitter cold—some were wearing figure skates, some
had hockey gear, all twenty-five of us were bent on cutting
a figure-eight the size of a horse corral into the frozen river.
A boy was carving an acrostic in the ice that said the world,
at rest, was better now than ever in the past. But who knew?

This chilling air was not of our making, nor was it the last.
Up Library Lane, the town's young teens arrived in packs,
my sister showing a flair for pirouettes. Like Dutch gliders,
we dreamed it was the Middle Ages, the Thames all frozen
over, busy with carts or horses everywhere, snowball fights,
mince pie stands, dogs, bears, stories of a falconer who fell
through to the murky bottom. At eight or nine years old, we

couldn't know our fate except by moving in concentric circles.
There were bonfires on the ice, stout fishermen, donut stands,
a snowman looking like a yeti, a lady with battery-heated socks
and, as in a Bruegel winter scene, a child peering out behind
a mask of death. The ink-black ice was glass-like, I'd skate far
and long till not a soul was anywhere in sight, only lake trout
swimming slowly and the drowned man floating down below.

History of the Palatines

We're dumbstruck that having left the city's melting pot
we're surrounded now by churches, farms or burial plots
belonging to your folk, emigrants from Rheinland-Pfalz,

close to where you grew up in a valley in the Sauerland.
Towns nearby have quirky names, as we learn about
a colony's refugee calamity, like one that we have now.

We meet in Germantown, where egrets are nesting in
the park, Otto's Market's packed as we wait for bread
to be delivered from across the river near West Camp,

Saugerties, where the Palatine affair began with a book
of names for settlers who endured the bitter winter
of 1708, when a Holy Roman Empire was becoming

something else that had little to do with principalities,
guilds, banking, nation-states, in a year when blackbirds
froze mid-air, wines seized up in barrels and our herds

froze to death in barns. The Palatines along the Rhine,
crushed by the French, their own princes, too, accepted
Queen Anne's offer of assistance, poled their makeshift

rafts on icy rivers down to Rotterdam, boarding ships
to reach the Blackheath camps for the destitute, infirm,
at 30,000 strong. From London, many made their way

to Ireland and the colonies of Carolina and New York,
up the Hudson to where they worked to process tar
from sparse white pines (with little rich or gluey pitch)

and live indentured to the crown in cabins owned
by Robert Livingston, to burn hollows, cut trees,
to open up roads and fields for British naval stores.

Land-lease wasn't liberty in this land where farmers
were on their own. Some say wealthy Mohawks saw
their plight, gave them pasture-place on the Schoharie,

some came to us in Rhinebeck to till the rocky soil.
Others moved out to Amish counties, where we've
gone to eat sour cheese and red beet eggs for lunch.

Poplar Forest

We scour the Blue Ridge Parkway, eager
to spot a feral pig, bristly boars that tore
up farmer's fields for several centuries,

separating north from south, town from
town, as tempers flare again at rallies for
the Christian right, for bump-stock guns,

against banned books, a politics of woke,
as we look for the lost colony at Roanoke,
imagine being Jefferson or Sally Hemings,

extolling human dignity yet forcing girls to
servitude, puzzling over fossil mastodons,
a race of giants from the Bible. There was

no view on what extinction was, no study
of bedrock layers, but territorial imperative
was god, as genocide was justified to tame

the wilderness, cursing tribes in the name
of nations. As we drive to Big Bone Lick,
Kentucky, we pass through Poplar Forest,

a hideaway for a third President, his home
an octagon or boiling pit for radical ideas,
Palladio's designs, an enlightened curiosity.

The estate was far from public life, where
shackled men grew wheat or tobacco seed
for family profit. In truth, our democratic

lands were still a long way off, as we find
a way to a little liberty, equality, fraternity
stewing in the roots beneath the poplars.

The Oblong

Before the Revolution, the colonies in
what's called 'a land of steady habits'

claimed turf beyond the marshes of
Long Island, up the Hudson, even

straight out to Iowa and the Pacific.
No one bothered to ask inhabitants,

Mashantucket Pequots, Naugatucks,
Mohegans, not to mention Quakers

or those of lesser faith. In faith, tracts
of land from dukes, counts, did count

and little more. Now a panhandle holds
shoreline, in exchange for a New York

two-mile strip up Harlem Valley towards
infinity. We walk the railroad beds where

farmers traded corn for cabbage or sent
their milk cows upstate to people with

no (recorded) past. We slog into a Great
Swamp watershed, as mosquitos feast on

minks. It's spring, there are spicy pinks
and the ferns have overgrown the gravel

spur to a south woods trail. We rail against
taxes or tribulations of the rich and stumble

into a ditch of spikenard. A pall in pastures
and parking lots, as we work to salvage car

parts from an over-quarried Purgatory Hill.
Here in a hardwood forest of black locust,

I can feel the rise and fall of the Taconics,
the breathing of a molten core beneath us

as it sighs and primes us with the patience
of geologic time for our eventual undoing.

The Goblet of the Titans

Erratic boulders crowd the foreground of a painting
that tries to crystallize a century of expansion into
woodland habitats and hues. It's aiming to expose
the fashionable *nature morte* for what it is, pure pride

in things, weirdly out of place in a fiery wilderness.
A giant goblet, neoclassical, dominates a mountain
valley where it's rained; everything's soaked in dew.
A Tuscan lake's atop the urn, an allegory of a sort

for the western frontier of 1833. Sailboats pass by
ornamental gardens as if there's never been a war
or bloodshed on the European continent, where
the painter, Thomas Cole, visited to hone his craft

of dark and sultry vistas of the American baroque.
Back in his studio, eerie echoes fill the Catskills,
his life's mission was to posit a philosophy for
death or immortality, where he foists a Bosch's

garden of delights on the sedentary landscape
of New York State. Some gods or giants must
have wandered through the wilderness and left
this favored cup before they disappeared forever.

Hudson, Whaling City

Crows flock to the Rip Van Winkle Bridge,
into a stubble field in a factory town that's
seen its better days, second graders waiting
for a school bell. On bluestone sidewalks,
people off a train are eyeing woolen goods.

An antique warehouse hides a whaleboat's
wreckage, its try-pots, fluke spades, bones
of a leviathan, stripped for oil or ambergris.
Here were the origins of window shopping,
women's shuttle looms knocking into night.

Motorcycles throttle up and race from boat
docks to the eastern hills, where curlews lay
their eggs in open grasslands. Here markets
hosted auction blocks for human suffering,
now designer showrooms, fancy shoe-stores

by the Whaler Inn. Bluish thunderheads
gather above the mountains. The red-light
district flourished for near a hundred years,
now our daughters selling baskets made in
Tripoli, Kampala and Macau, commanding

monstrous markups for the haute bourgeois
who've fattened on blubber of the fin whale.
Today, we walk a mile of shops with friends
from Cincinnati, watch a sturgeon as it leaps
out of the river running fast down to the sea.

Earth Day, 2024

Coffee with Norman at Astro Place—
as he called it—having set a libretto
and a book of poems here, a bright
biopic on RFK and a utopian play

about our nation if Gore had won.
I dream I pass a billboard of Trujillo
advertising the 1939 World's Fair,
I cherish a lifetime of meetups as

when we shared an Amontillado
beside the hidden wall where Poe
entombed an enemy combatant.
Bookstalls with Balzac, Hugo, Zola

wearing down old Fourth Avenue
where Bartleby and Melville's aunt
would be huffing up the boulevard,
all the way north to Seneca Village.

But here on St. Mark's, the lindens
are in full bloom at Cooper Union,
where once you visited my class
to read your 'Gloucester's Eyes.'

Artists and anarchists vouchsafe
this tiny schist of earth, keeping it
intact until the blustering politicians
cease, desist, so we can live in peace.

Part Five: Nature

Salamander Crossing

Nature takes us by surprise this winter when it's mild enough
and raining, suddenly there's congestion on a county road, as
amphibians, red efts and tree frogs, migrate from the woods
to vernal pools. A Jefferson's salamander seems unsure which
way to go across the asphalt, with oncoming cars at midnight.

A crowd of volunteers is there with day-glow vests and torches,
quick to coax the critters off the tar and into a culvert where
coltsfoot is cropping up. All at once, a flock of crested turkeys
saunters from a cornfield, careful on the shoulder to sidestep
any single-minded, self-directed wood frogs or spring peepers.

Is there a moral to the story? A mother hen gets side-swiped
by a pickup truck, while over twenty eastern newts, chorus
frogs and toads get saved by the overeager lot that's brought
their sensibilities to bear so early in the season on this balmy
night when I thought to join them but was better off in bed.

—for Aesop

The Thirteenth Lake

Deep in the Adirondacks, a washed-out garnet mine
is languishing despite a perky tourist trade that
tries to buff up business with earrings, studs
and tales of gems from the bottom of a sea.
Just miles from the trickling Mahicantuck,
Thirteenth Lake won't give up its secrets,
not the sunken airplane forty feet below

nor any boiler swill from dilapidated mills
on its pristine banks. Rather the waters speak
with some deep intelligence that's transported
by a meteor from across a galaxy to find one
random friendly human being who's worthy
of a sacrifice in the name of timber wolves.
Let it be so, its waters flooding up to heaven.

Landscape, Three Cows

The ghosts of trees surround the Housatonic,
cottonwoods and ginkgos, pin oaks, sugar maples,
honey locusts, stick-like trunks that dance along a northern
fence, bottle-brush cell towers like maritime pines, fire lookouts,
windsocks. In a rickety old duck blind, an artist is painting cows
at sunset, when the fields are ablaze with columbines.
Souped-up cars drive by outside the picture plane,

hemlocks sprout, deep in loam like shoots of grape,
crows are picking at a carcass in an oxbow of the river.
A watercolor sketch is lying, greenish white, in orchard grass
under a migratory flyway, where a farmer tramps up hills
towards home, up stone walls, one field at a time,
as the painter daubs at shadows of three cows
that are settling down in hay for moonrise.

—after Milton Avery

Cicadas

This time the 17-year and 13-year broods
arrive in tandem, to make a racket only
racoons tolerate. Below Blacksburg in
Virginia, one year they broke through
the earth like the dead from graves.
We were artists there, fussing with
projects of the heart or biking deep
into pastures of grazing sheep, lying
by a river where worlds burst into
bloom a hundred years ago, and now
again in June. Under a full moon, at
once, cicadas came, honed their wings
of carbon steel so we couldn't sleep,
elms agitated by the noise. Boys took
sticks to swat them down, crush them
into pulp, as in Elysian fields bursting
with locusts rioting. *A plague upon all*
artists, they seem to be saying, seething
or screeching as we finished our poems
and our prints, sprinting through their
dim cacophony to reach the judges' table.

Out Eeling

We meet at an eco-research lab, below
eel ladders on a dam whose watershed
is full of streams with names of farms
or vanished languages or rocky bluffs.
Today we go for fun, pull on green
waders, grab buckets, logbooks, fish
line to count eels caught in a fyke net.
We go with eeler Izzy, lover of biology,
as two great herons stand in the shallows
turned to stone. We're making waves like
the eels do, sloshing, paddling backwards,
catadromous, ecstatic, splashing in fresh
waters, the eels not yet male or female,
not ready to return to spawning grounds.

The three of us watch damselflies dart by,
with just a few stragglers in the eel mop,
determined to survive a sixth extinction.
You put an arm around my shoulders for
a photo—you, a shiny glass eel that's all
grown up, and me, yanked and yellowed
into a silver eel that may just live forever
like its kin the spiny eel, the Japanese eel
of the Kuroshio currents of the Pacific.
It's a habit of mind to trace your steps,
shifting in murky waters. Suddenly, as if
out of air, gangs of elvers are sliding past
as if the end of time was near at hand, to
find a spot where storms can't hurt them.

Soundscape Pando

A quaking aspen entity of 50,000 trees
in a fish lake forest in central Utah,
where a litter of kit foxes snore
where black ants are on the march
where crickets rub sore legs together
where desert winds are whispering
where tree frogs serenade the moon
where grackles congregate in corn
where spiders spin a woven orb
where mass tugs more than gravity
where shadows in the saplings sing
where butterflies beget new sorrows
where mason bees are sipping nectar
where rain arrives in thunderstorms
where deer are ravaging a forest floor
where the sun comes up upon a hill
where rangers douse a surface fire
where swallows gorge on stable flies
where snow is carpeting the sedge
where gravel runs down rivulets
where a bear enjoys a clover honey
where minks are running for their lives
where petals of the water lily drop
where we record the aspens quivering,
each one of them connected underneath.

On the Esopus

From outer space, if you could see
the Esopus, it might look like a serpent,
its headwaters in a lake at Winnisook, not too
far from Neversink, the crater of Panther Mountain
and its slide down to the sea. We camp here one Thanksgiving,
a stone's throw from a meth lab and broken-down cabins
for vacationers from before the jet age. Once there

was smallpox here and people fished for fluke
and warmed up venison. Now the river has
the sheen of summer and an eagle flies
close to the mirrored surface after pike.
Every particle of rock and sand and clay
is flowing towards its intended destination,
except for rotten snags of trees that turn to soot.

Reading Mary Oliver

I'm reading Mary Oliver
in our art delivery truck
near Lexington and 59th,

an *Araneus juniperi* ticks
across the dashboard,
oblivious to our pangs

of hunger, a green glass
scarab who must have
joined us in the Bronx.

The insect's shadow traces
words in a book of poems
that fetishizes sky, black

oaks, bronze fruit, starlings
in the winter of my death.
I'm twenty-eight this week

and envy the crawler's poise,
as grand as any giant squid.
As I scribble notes, I lose

sight of her, as she skitters
down a page and floats away
in the direction of a trattoria.

Capybara Ocean

If I was naming the open seas, I'd be sure to call one
Capybara Ocean. In truth, my daughter thought of it.
By way of her endless drawings, her love for animals,
her non-stop animations full of heart and humor,
she squints her eyes, puts a finger down someplace
on an undiscovered shore and scribbles out a reddish
rodent at a delta of the Essequibo River, where bugs

are giant-sized and forest creatures on Sloth Island
dream of a time when we knew what friendship was.
Madly, she draws with colored pencils an easy-going,
warm and fuzzy jungle rat, or whole families as they
lounge about a riverbank and bob below the waves.
And I find myself most tickled by the oddest notion
from an anthropologist in Haifa—that it was wheat

that domesticated us and not the other way around.
If we're to survive our catastrophic climate change
we'll have to do it with a scientific grace for those
who've made it with us this far—giraffes and deer,
monarch butterflies and bees, all of the passengers
on our fateful ark, like baby capybaras at the ocean,
whose job is to unwind and take it one day at a time.

—for Lotti

Clouds

... strangely, you look around and above you
every morning to see whether mist falls or rises
J. W. Goethe

I'm sitting by his *sommergartenhaus* in spring
at noon with friends and good Italian coffee.
We've planned an exhibition based on plant
charts the master poet, playwright, gardener
has hung in an alcove of his Mephistophelian
cottage. Post-modern, fragmentary, his notes
unpack any semblance of the whole, of demi-

gods or destiny, symmetry or the holy cattle
we can see from the terrace where we relax.
A taxonomy of clouds, you tease, is a place
to start defining the beginning of the end,
as scuds blow in, widen, shifting, looming,
gay and hopeful, full of a light that we find
inside ourselves when we sit back and listen.

The Far Field

Deep in uptown traffic in the Bronx,
I'm in a panic in the pounding rain,
my GPS is pointing me away
from Yonkers, towards
the western meadowlands,
the great gray bridge instead
of up the Saw Mill River.

With no place to turn around
in rush-hour gridlock, I comply,
heading out beyond the Palisades as if
I might drive across the country.
Eventually, I figure out that time's
trumped distance, my route's
been redirected because
of a massive pileup at a rotary.

In an hour I'm on a thruway north,
thunderheads drifting in currents
of cold air, the sun
is reappearing, the suburbs
no longer in my rear-view mirror.

The day begins to fade
as I speed past toll roads, flocks
of sheep along the river, cars stalled,
broken down on the pot-holed
turnpike leading to summer's end.
After weeks in the ICU with you,
I'd come to understand the rifts
between us, gaps love chiseled

into fevered consciousness
as I kissed you on the cheek
and set back off for home,
sure that you were out of danger.

My brother calls to say our mom
would pass away that night. I felt like
I was sliding off a spinning planet,
pausing at a truck stop that fenced
in fields of sunflowers. I stopped
to call her, to read Ecclesiastes
and a Roethke poem she gave
me when I was twelve, one that
set my life of the spirit into gear.

Radio Woodstock came in range,
Pete Seeger singing 'to everything
there is a season,' for no
good reason I began to cry
and turned to breathing as if
I'd been hurled to outer space.

The aftershock hit home, October 7th
was the day you almost died, the day
of massacres in Israel, a tragedy of war
and genocide in Palestine. I lost colleagues
there and helped my friend in getting
out of Gaza, by taking a job in Spain.
I sat there dumb for hours as stars
came out across that faraway,

alien rest-stop meadow full of rue,
as I broke down and knew
in my heart that Mom was gone
and that you would be okay.

I remember driving with Mom
to the Jemez mountains, sitting in
a kitchen with whiskey and no place
we had to go. At our daughter's birth
I caught her looking in a mirror
furtively at us. Her marriages
were rocky, she smiled and carried
on, with a grace I try to emulate,
with a tangential, spacey logic
I've inherited from her, a breadth
of vision that reminds me of
that bison grazing on a mesa top,
looking out across Nebraska prairie
as we drove across the plains.

Did we ever get to the ghost ranch
of the man who fell to Earth
(as both of us loved David Bowie),
when she left us kids for a whole
new life, we five landing on our feet?
We hiked in Mesa Verde, Bandolier,
threw clay pots, read Rilke's letters
and prized the power of the word.

When I was six, she and I would clean
a hay barn by ourselves, we'd sit
by Lieutenant River cattails or stroll
on Commerce St., New York City.
I remember her huffing father
down in a cellar off a granite ledge,
fumes of heating oil, pipes that burst
below a lacy-curtained bedroom nestled
in the giant boulders by the roof.

I remember reading picture books
aloud with brothers in the afternoon,
sitting on his veranda, on a swing set
lost in musty violets, on a seesaw
angled up to rocket to the moon.

A forgotten sandbox, an uncle's
stuttering, beat-up shutters banging
on a beach house door, cattle dogs
as subjects of polite discussion—
birdsong, planting grapevines
or reflecting on New England's
sordid trafficking of human souls.

Walking to a village for penny candy,
past graves of aunts I didn't know,
Mom showed up to hear my high school
graduation speech (fifty years ago
I wrote that there's hope for us yet),
my sister napping in a corner of a tent.

But is it now a time to weep, to heal,
to sow, recoup or reap? Is it a time to laugh
or sigh, a season for all things revealed
in this faraway field of yarrow?

We say that Mom was there for us,
but always a million miles away,
a body of still water, a sandbar
in the murky dark, her watercolors
capturing transparency and light.

I dream I'm in a great stone fortress
as choral music plays, as I find a place
to sail back down to where her
mind might meet with mine,
so alike but sure to trickle down
as infinitely separate cataracts.

She was nurturing for sure, she had
an easy-morning smile, staring out
at offshore wind farms, looking for
the horizontal. Here in this far field,
in a stream of traffic and emissions,
a marshy bog and creeks meandering

until they reach an estuary mouth.
She's waiting to be held in someone's
arms, just as she cradled me the day
I came into this world of shrikes
that terrify the June bugs, the sun

warming the earth, hills along a lake
eroding the dust, where I find
in the grass some words
for her as she makes
her way amidst the waves
to her people in the sky.

The far field is as close
as a whisper in her ear:
now it's time to turn towards
the sea, the end of everything is here.

—for Barbara

Acknowledgements

Thanks to the editors of *The Nature of Our Times* for publishing "Soundscape Pando." Thanks to the Virginia Center for the Creative Arts and to the Bard Ecology Field Station in Annandale-on-Hudson, NY. Thanks to Norman MacAfee and Miguel Cervantes, Michael Dinwiddie, Patricia Spears Jones, Emily Knight, Kevin Boyle, Marjory Wentworth, Ruth Danon, Elaine Sexton, Michelle Montalbano, Tiffany Troy, Akiko Busch, Phil Pardi, Mark Patsfall and Sarah Young, Jochen Saueracker and Birgit Jensen, Mike Glier, Sean Bayliss and Alexandra Keiser, Jon Conroe, Devek Singh, Laurie Husted and the gang on the Red Hook Conservation Advisory Council, my brothers John and Ted as well as Barbara (Westermann) and Lotte (Allen) for their support or careful reading of the poems.

About the Author

Bill's work echoes beloved voices from poetry, poets, history and politics and a look at the natural world in an era of climate action, with personal memories and a fervent look into language, love and the ties that bind us to each other. There's humor, humanism, a music of the earth, irreverence, a quest for ethical answers in a world titling off its axis. Poems echo Lowell and Bishop, Pasolini, Philip Levine and Muriel Rukeyser, with their spirits of questioning and grace. Also a visual artist, Bill's work can be seen at www.ekphrases.com.

He is the recipient of a 2009 National Endowment for the Arts fellowship in Creative Writing and has published five previous books of poems. Bill worked at the United Nations in New York in writing and technology communications for many years after teaching at Cooper Union and the School of Visual Arts, hoping to bring a poetry of humanism and heart to the poetry canon. He's currently working with a conservation advisory group to explore and inventory Hudson Valley local habitats and climate needs.

www.ingramcontent.com/pod-product-compliance
Lightning Source LLC
Chambersburg PA
CBHW021338060726
47591CB00006B/2073

* 9 7 8 1 9 6 9 9 0 0 2 0 4 *